Blockchain
The Beginners Guide To Understanding The Technology Behind Bitcoin & Cryptocurrency

Artemis Caro

Copyright © 2017 Artemis Caro

All rights reserved.

INTRODUCTION

As cryptocurrencies like Bitcoin gain popularity around the world, a considerable uptick in attention from mainstream media outlets has brought the term "blockchain" out of obscurity and into the spotlight. "Blockchain" has even become a bit of a buzzword in the tech and financial sectors, and increasingly in other fields and industries.

There is a lot of hype surrounding the concept of the blockchain, but what does this term actually *mean*? What is blockchain technology? What does it do? How does it work? Why does it matter? These questions are not always answered with due diligence in the sea of headlines and "think pieces" that deal with digital currencies and other applications using blockchains. As a result, many people are left with an incomplete understanding of this transformative new technology and its implications for the future.

One challenge when learning about blockchains is that much of the real power behind the scenes of this technology involves complex mathematical processes that can be difficult to grasp for those of us who do not have advanced degrees in computer science or a background in cryptography. Unless you plan to become a developer and build your own blockchain applications, however, you can gain a thorough understanding of how blockchains work on a practical level without needing to tackle any algorithms.

The goal of this book is not to plumb the depths of the mathematical wizardry used to code blockchain-based applications, but rather to serve as an introduction to the broader architecture and conceptual background behind blockchain technology. We will take a practical approach, examining how blockchains are used in the real world, how they work, and why this technology is being hailed as revolutionary by many prominent voices around the world.

When the Internet arrived, it completely transformed the structure of daily life across the globe. Many people believe that the implications of blockchain technology will give rise to a paradigm shift of similar scale. Blockchain is a foundational technology that has the potential to reshape the nature of institutions, industries, and the global economy. Before we set the world on fire, however, let's get back to the basics: what is a blockchain, how does it work, and what exactly does it do? These are some of the fundamental questions we will set out to answer throughout the course of this book. First, however, as we begin to explore this technology of the future, it is helpful to get an overview of its past. Where did the idea of blockchain come from?

CONTENTS

	Introduction	i
1	**A Brief History of Blockchain Technology**	1
2	**Blockchain Basics: Managing Digital Transactions**	3
	1) How We Handle Financial Transactions	4
	2) What is a Distributed Ledger?	5
3	**The SHA-256 Hashing Algorithm**	11
	1) The Role of Bitcoin Miners	14
	2) Bitcoin Miners Pay to Play	16
	3) Blockchain Beyond Bitcoin	18
4	**Cryptocurrency Beyond Bitcoin**	20
	1) Ethereum	20
	2) Golem	24
	3) Ripple	25
5	**Implications Of Blockchain: Big Data, Privacy & Personal Data**	27
	1) Profiting from Blockchain Technologies	31
	2) Limitations & Challenges of Blockchain	38
	3) Quantum Computing	41
6	**The Human Touch: Or, The 51% Problem**	43
	1) The Future of Blockchain	45
	Conclusion	47

CHAPTER 1
A BRIEF HISTORY OF BLOCKCHAIN TECHNOLOGY

The concept of a "blockchain" was introduced in 2008 by Satoshi Nakamoto as part of the protocol behind the digital currency Bitcoin. Nakamoto published a technical paper to an email list that was popular amongst cryptography enthusiasts that laid out the basic principles behind both Bitcoin, a digital currency, and the blockchain, the *underlying technology* behind that currency.

Shortly thereafter, in 2009, the first blockchain was put into implementation when the first Bitcoin was mined by Nakamoto and put into circulation. Today, Bitcoin has achieved global renown and is accepted as a valid currency by increasingly more vendors. You can buy everything from airline tickets to online courses using Bitcoin; even Burger King has started to accept it!

Over the past decade, many other digital currencies, often called "cryptocurrencies," have emerged utilizing blockchain technology to manage transactions. We will look at some of these in subsequent chapters of this book, but it is important to keep in mind that the implications of blockchain technology reach far beyond the realm of digital currencies.

While cryptocurrencies, and specifically Bitcoin, were the first applications to use blockchains, many industries are beginning to explore blockchain tech as a way to handle a wide range of procedures, including smart contracts, data storage, and resource management. Throughout this book, we will look at several different ways that blockchain applications are being developed both pertaining to cryptocurrencies and in other fields.

Anecdotally, one of the more fascinating details in the history of blockchain technology is the identity of its creator. Although there are many theories, nobody has ever uncovered the true identity of Satoshi Nakamoto. Whether Nakamoto is an individual or a group of people, we may never know. What is certain, however, is that their contribution to the future of technology is incredibly significant. Many prominent thinkers and voices from within the tech industry see revolutionary potential for blockchain technology, and with good reason!

CHAPTER 2
BLOCKCHAIN BASICS; MANAGING DIGITAL TRANSACTIONS

There are several underlying concepts that make blockchain technology uniquely suited to handle digital transactions. Today, the most well-known and widely implemented application of blockchains is found in the cryptocurrency space, where blockchains are used to handle financial transactions that happen digitally on a peer-to-peer basis.

While the applications for blockchain technology are not limited exclusively to digital financial transactions, this is a good place to begin exploring how blockchains work in a real-world context. Digital currencies, pioneered by Bitcoin, have emerged as a new asset class, which is remarkable in and of itself. Beyond the emergence of digital assets, the blockchain framework also provides a model for rethinking institutional structures in terms of how power is organized and value is distributed. We are still in the early stages of exploring the possibilities for blockchain technology, but the space is developing quickly. It is not an understatement to suggest that blockchain technology will fundamentally reshape the nature of governments, personal property, and the global economy within the next decade.

In order to get a clearer picture of how blockchains work, it is helpful to begin by looking at digital currencies, like Bitcoin. Digital currencies are, as of now, the most well established implementations of functioning blockchains. In the case of digital currencies, or "cryptocurrencies," blockchain technology is used to handle financial transactions. Before we look at how the blockchain model works, it is helpful to look at how financial transactions have worked historically.

How We Handle Financial Transactions

For centuries, people have relied on centralized institutions like banks and governments to serve as intermediaries when it comes to storing and transacting financial assets.

As a practical matter, most people keep the majority of their finances stored in a bank. There are many advantages to this. If, for example, you had your entire life savings buried under the floorboards of your house and your house burned down, you would be in big trouble. Banks provide a promise of security, protecting your assets in exchange for various transaction fees. We trust banks to keep our funds secure in exchange for a percentage of our money. Over time, this model of keeping money in banks emerged as the norm. In an increasingly digital world, however, many people have begun to search for alternatives to the historical model of consolidating resources in centralized institutions.

Today, as more and more transactions take place digitally, the need for trust and security has become even more significant. Financial information exists largely as data, and transactions are ultimately just file transfers.

Without a secure process, it is incredibly easy to manipulate data. Hackers regularly compromise bank servers, ATM machines, and other places where financial data is stored or transactions occur.

One of the biggest challenges of managing financial transactions on a peer-to-peer basis is the "double-spending problem," or how to ensure that someone isn't spending the same money twice. When Bitcoin arrived on the scene, it offered a solution to this problem, enabling direct peer-to-peer transactions to take place in a secure way that did not require trust from either party or a third-party intermediary, like a bank. That solution was the blockchain.

What is a Distributed Ledger?

While Bitcoin paved the way blockchain technology, many subsequent applications, including but not limited to other digital currencies, have been built on the blockchain framework. One of the fundamental concepts driving the success of blockchain technology is its use of a distributed ledger system.

Ok, so what is a distributed ledger? Basically, a distributed ledger is exactly what it sounds like. A ledger is just list of records. Instead of keeping this list in one place, a *distributed ledger* is stored in many different locations simultaneously. Not all forms of distributed ledgers are blockchains, but all blockchains use some version of a distributed ledger.

Decentralization is one of the core concepts behind blockchain. By keeping multiple copies of the record of transactions in different locations all across the world, visible to anyone, the need for a "trusted" third party institution to serve as a middleman and oversee transactions is eliminated.

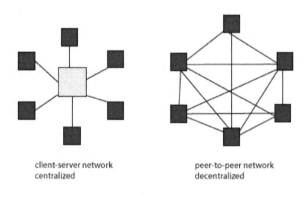

client-server network
centralized

peer-to-peer network
decentralized

To delve a bit deeper into how distributed ledgers work, let's imagine a hypothetical situation: pretend you have a big three-ring binder where you write down every financial transaction you make in a year. Any time you make money or spend money, you write down the details in this binder. Only one binder exists and you keep it in your desk. A lot of things could go wrong in this scenario: your house could burn down, a nefarious person could sneak in and tamper with the information, you could forget to include a few documents and end up with numbers that don't add up, or any number of other unfortunate mishaps.

Instead of having only one binder, imagine that hundreds of thousands of identical copies of this same binder existed in desks of people all across the world. Every time any detail was added into the binder, the information would have to be checked against all of the copies to make sure that the numbers added up correctly, and the new information would be added into all of them at once. If once binder contained a transaction that didn't show up in any of the others, we could assume that binder was faulty. Now, in order for someone to tamper with your information, they would have to tamper with every single one of these binders all over the world at the same time.

Obviously, using a system of binders in desks is not very practical. In the virtual world, however, this is actually somewhat similar to how a distributed ledger works. In blockchains, each individual transaction, no matter how big or small, is recorded in a "block."

Each block contains a special timestamp that links it to the previous block. This allows computers to check each proposed transaction against the previous one. If the timestamps do not add up properly across the majority of computers, the transaction will be rejected. If the majority agrees that the proposed transaction is valid, it will be verified and added into a new block in the chain, or a new record in the ledger. Now, the next proposed transaction will be checked against that block's timestamp, and so forth.

In order for someone, such as a hacker, to enter false

information into the blockchain, they would have to alter the information not only on one block, but on every single block on the entire blockchain simultaneously across the majority of participating computers all over the world. Even with current technology, to accomplish that would require such a massive amount of computing power that it is effectively an impossible feat. Thus, the blockchain's distributed ledger system is secure by design.

Because each transaction is checked against the entire history of previous transactions by multiple machines all distributed all over the world, it is impossible for someone to "cheat" the blockchain by attempting to spend the same money twice. One of the transactions will not match with the historical record, and it will be rejected as invalid.

Not only is the "double spending" problem solved but transactions do not require either party to trust the other or a third party institution in order to be conducted. Person A cannot claim that they sent Person B money that "got lost in the mail" and Person B cannot claim that they "never received the money." All transactions are publicly visible, and therefore both parties will be able to see a record of the transaction on the blockchain.

Blockchain and Bitcoin

One of the most confusing and misunderstood aspects of blockchain, as a concept, comes when we try to uncouple it from Bitcoin. As stated previously, Bitcoin is simply one application built on a blockchain framework. It is also the first, largest, and most well known functioning open blockchain in the world. Bitcoin's implementation of blockchain technology is often cited as definitive, meaning that when people say "blockchain" they are often talking specifically about the blockchain model used by Bitcoin.

It is important to understand that the Bitcoin model is not definitive of blockchain technology. Bitcoin demonstrates *one* implementation of this technology. There are several factors that make Bitcoin's blockchain work the way that it does, and it is worth examining each of them to get a fuller understand of which aspects of Bitcoin's implementation of the blockchain are specific to Bitcoin and which are aspects of blockchain technology in general.

The Bitcoin Blockchain

There are several fundamental concepts that work together to create a blockchain ecosystem that is unique to Bitcoin. Other cryptocurrencies have implemented similar models, but for our purposes it makes sense to zoom in on Bitcoin and break down how the Bitcoin blockchain works.

We already know that blockchains are a form of distributed ledger. If we dig a bit deeper into this idea of a distributed ledger, some questions that may arise are: how are transactions are verified? Who records them? How we can be sure this information is accurate?

Encryption

If you recall from the earlier section on the history of Bitcoin, you may remember that the concept was introduced initially to a popular cryptography mailing list. Why cryptography?

The field of cryptography has developed rapidly alongside digital technology as a way securing information. Cryptography has traditionally been a somewhat obscure field, historically used largely in military contexts. In the days of the Roman Empire, Julias Cesar famously used an encryption technique to send coded messages to his generals.

In the digital age, encryption has become a fundamental part of everyday life. As hacking and identity theft have become more and more prominent, basic encryption practices have entered the mainstream as protective measures for keeping one's personal data safe. Whether we are aware of it or not, most of us today are already familiar with basic encryption techniques, such as using passwords to access our email accounts or enabling two-factor authentication on our smartphones. Most of rely on encrypted transactions on a regular basis, from making online purchases to accessing our bank accounts.

It should come as no surprise then, that Bitcoin relies on cryptographically secure algorithms to validate transactions and manage the blockchain.

CHAPTER 3
THE SHA-256 HASHING ALGORITHM

Bitcoin uses a cryptographically secure SHA-256 hashing algorithm. While an in-depth explanation of exactly how this works is beyond the scope of this book, it is helpful to get a basic overview. One way to think of this is to imagine a black box. That box is the SHA-256 algorithm. For our purposes, we aren't really going to worry about what happens inside the box, the nuts and bolts of the algorithm itself. We will just proceed with the assumption that inside the box, mysterious mathematical things happen.

The important aspect, for us, is that you can take any kind of data, of any size, and feed it into the box. Ultimately all digital data, even complex things like movies that are many gigabytes in size, exist as a sequence of 1's and 0's, or "bits." When we feed any kind of data into the black box of SHA-256, the bits in that data are processed. We can think of the bits as being "rearranged" in a certain way inside the box. When the data has been processed by the black box, it spits out a 256-bit string of seemingly random characters, which looks like nonsense. We can think of this string like a unique "fingerprint" representing the exact data that we fed in.

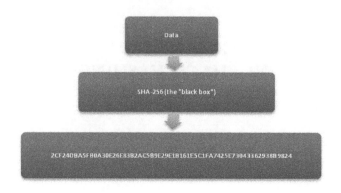

(The Data here is the word "hello" hashed using SHA-256)

Truth be told, the apparent "nonsense" that comes out is not actually nonsense. SHA-256 is *determinative*, which means that if you put the same data into the "black box", you will get the same exact output string, or "fingerprint", every single time. If you apply SHA-256 the word "hello" you will get the identical 64-character string as seen above.

Another feature of this hash function is that it is a *one-way function*. This means that you cannot take the output string and convert it back to the original data. So, in our example, we cannot reverse the process by using the "nonsense" to get back to the original "hello."

One example of how this is used is to verify documents, such as PDF's. If you sign a contract and send it to someone along with the SHA-256 fingerprint, they can test the hash to ensure that not a single bit of the data has been altered. If they feed the document into SHA-256 and get the identical output string, then the document has not been changed.

If, on the other hand, the slightest change has occurred- regardless of whether it was a well-intentioned modification such as a typo being fixed or a case of nefarious tampering - the fingerprint that comes out will be completely different. The nature or scope of the change to the original data doesn't matter to the algorithm; the output of the SHA-256 algorithm will be totally different unless the data is 100% identical. For example, in the above example, if you change the word "hello" to "Hello" or "HELLO," you will get a totally different output string.

Now that we have a basic grasp on how SHA-256 works you might be wondering how this relates to the Bitcoin blockchain. This can be one of the more complicated concepts to grasp in terms of what goes on under the hood of Bitcoin's protocol. In order to understand the role of SHA-256 in the "Proof of Work" model that makes Bitcoin function, we need to dig a bit deeper into how Bitcoin miners participate in the blockchain ecosystem.

The Role of Bitcoin Miners

Many explanations of how Bitcoin transactions are verified say something akin to: "miners solve complicated math problems to add blocks to the chain in exchange for a reward." This is accurate, and it is a fine explanation in terms of getting the big-picture. When it comes to understanding the larger architecture of blockchain technology as it applies to Bitcoin, however, we find that this explanation is a bit oversimplified. For our purposes, we need to explore the mechanics of Bitcoin mining a bit more closely.

Mining involves complex computation designed to find certain combinations of random numbers (called "nonces"). These nonces are combined with information about particular Bitcoin transactions to yield a SHA-256 string that meets very specific criteria.

Data concerning Bitcoin transactions is found in the header, or first "chunk" of any block on the blockchain, which is displayed as a SHA-256 string. So, the first "chunk" of the string that makes up each block contains information about the transactions contained in that block, such as the time, amount of Bitcoin, addresses involved, and other details. The remainder of the string is produced by finding a nonce that, when added to the transaction data, will produce a SHA-256 string that meets the aforementioned target criteria.

So, what is this criteria and who decides it? Bitcoin blocks need to be constructed according to a set of rules in order to be considered valid by the consensus model governing all "nodes" on the Bitcoin network. This rule set- the criteria that must be met to generate a valid block- is written into the core code of Bitcoin's software. The "rules" are a set of functions written into the C++ code that runs on every machine (or "node") that is connected to the Bitcoin network.

A miner needs to create a block following this set of rules. First, the block needs to include information about the most recent Bitcoin transactions. Then, the miner must find a nonce that, when added to the transaction data, will produce a SHA-256 string that meets the criteria set by Bitcoin's software (for example, the criteria might be something like the string must contain 15 zeroes in a row).

There is no way to find the nonce other than using a "brute force" method, which basically just means trial and error. Miners try a bunch of random numbers really quickly until they find one that works. When a miner "solves a block," it means that they have found a nonce that produces a SHA-256 hash that meets the criteria for a valid block. They can then submit their answer to the Bitcoin network and other nodes will check it and confirm that it is valid.

To give you an idea of how complicated it is to find the nonce, the Bitcoin network produces upwards of 500 quadrillion hashes per second. These are all attempts to find a nonce that produces the necessary result. Even with that massive amount of work, it still takes an average of 10 minutes to solve a block, or to find a viable nonce. When a miner does solve a block successfully, they are rewarded with a small amount of Bitcoin.

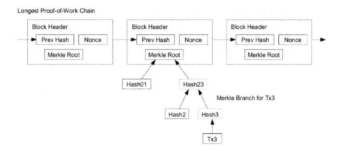

By Satoshi Nakamoto - http://bitcoin.org/bitcoin.pdf, MIT, https://commons.wikimedia.org/w/index.php?curid=24542868

(The "Merkle Root" is a reference to a mathematical concept called a Merkle Tree. In this case, the Merkle Root is the hash of all the transactions making up the block. The details of each individual transaction are also hashed, so the "Merkle Root" is actually the hash of all of those hashes.)

Bitcoin Miners Pay to Play

You may have heard people talk about Bitcoin mining as a way to make "free money." This has never been the case, even in the early days of Bitcoin, and it is even less so today as the complexity of solving blocks increases over time in correlation to the amount of Bitcoin in circulation.

The specificity of the SHA-256 string gets more complicated over time (this is known as the "difficulty target"), making the amount of power required to find a valid nonce more significant. Today, special equipment is needed to successfully mine Bitcoin in any sort of meaningful way, and even then most miners combine their resources into pools that share both the burden of work and the rewards.

Miners use their equipment to test hashes at an incredibly rapid rate. As you can imagine, this kind of computing power requires a lot of electricity, which is generally not free. The reason that the Bitcoin mining infrastructure works is due in part to the fact that to participate, miners incur a cost. Without the sacrifice, there is no reward. The only reason that someone would mine Bitcoin is because they believe the incentive is worth more than that hefty electric bill that comes from mining.

When a miner does find a nonce that works, their result will be checked and validated by the wider Bitcoin network. If it checks out, they have provided *Proof of Work* and can receive their reward. If the rest of the nodes on the Bitcoin network see that something in a proposed block does not meet the criteria, either by following a rule incorrectly or by failing to provide a nonce that meets the criteria, the block will be rejected and that miner will have just wasted money and resources. For example, if someone attempts to "double-spend," this will be caught and the block will be rejected.

Bitcoin's use of a Proof-of-Work consensus model makes it virtually impossible to cheat or hack the blockchain. With Bitcoin, miners pay to play, and it only pays to play fair. Not only that, but those who don't play fair will actually lose money due to the cost of electricity required to operate mining rigs.

Blockchain Beyond Bitcoin

When we look at the Bitcoin Blockchain, we can see that it is made up of several distinct parts that work together to create the overall architecture of the ecosystem. Three of the components that we have looked at thus far are the idea of a distributed ledger, the use of SHA-256, and a Proof-of-Work consensus model.

Which of these are unique to Bitcoin and which are baked into the concept of blockchain technology itself? That's a good question, and the answer may depend on whom you ask. There is some debate over where Bitcoin stops and blockchain begins, or rather what features of Bitcoin's blockchain are essential to creating other blockchains that actually work in a practical way.

On a basic level, when we remove the trappings of Bitcoin from the fundamental concept of a blockchain, we are left ultimately with the notion of a distributed ledger that contains a record of transactions. What kind of transactions and how they are handled, verified, and recorded is something that different blockchain applications may handle in different ways.

When we start to look into other implementations of blockchain technology, we need to look closely at how they function. How are they ensuring security? Are they open and accessible to anyone? Do they operate in a decentralized manner? How are they encrypting information? Are transactions anonymous? What kinds of transactions are being handled? Do they use Proof of Work? Is there another consensus model? These are all questions that arise when we begin to look at blockchain technology as it applies to spaces beyond Bitcoin.

CHAPTER 4
CRYPTOCURRENCY BEYOND BITCOIN

Ethereum

The cryptocurrency space is notoriously volatile. Things change on a daily basis and new coins are being developed all the time. What is considered revolutionary one day can be obsolete the next. That being said there are some digital currencies that have achieved relative stability. Bitcoin is widely considered to be the leader in blockchain-based currencies, but Ethereum has gained a lot of traction since its inception in late 2013.

Ethereum was developed by the programmer Vitalik Buterin. Unlike Bitcoin, which functions solely as a digital currency, Ethereum is a blockchain-based platform for developing decentralized applications that run using "smart contracts." Where Bitcoin serves an electronic peer-to-peer cash system, the Ethereum blockchain runs the code making up decentralized applications.

It may be helpful to visualize Ethereum as similar to a smartphone. A smartphone comes with a general operating system, like iOS or Android. Anybody can create apps that do any number of different things to run on that operating system. Ethereum, in this analogy, is like the operating system: a framework to build upon.

One application that runs on Ethereum is a digital currency, which is often also referred to as "Ethereum," although technically it is called Ether. This can be confusing, since both the currency and the platform are usually called "Ethereum," but it is important to remember that the currency is merely *one* aspect of the Ethereum blockchain framework. As a reward for maintaining the Ethereum blockchain, Ethereum "miners" are rewarded with Ether.

From its inception, Ethereum mining has worked on a Proof-of-Work consensus model similar to Bitcoin. As of 2017, however, the team behind Ethereum has announced plans to shift to a Proof-of-Stake model. Understanding the difference between these two systems of validating blockchain transactions is crucial to gaining context for some of the most pressing debates in the larger blockchain space today.

When we looked at "Proof of Work" as integral to the Bitcoin protocol, we covered how Bitcoin miners have to invest in special mining equipment that requires a lot of electricity to run in order to solve a block. Proof-of-Stake (PoS) works a bit differently.

A Proof-of-Stake model is a bit more like gambling. Rather than being called "miners," Ethereum is moving towards the term "validators." Validators *stake* a certain amount of their own money (Ether, in the case of Ethereum) towards solving a block. The more money a validator stakes, the higher the probability that they will solve the block.

In this example 4 validators are "staking" their own money towards solving a block. Validator 4 has the highest stake, and therefore the highest probability of solving the block and being rewarded.

The Proof-of-Stake model simulates the "work" involved with performing meaningless calculations, which thus reduces the real environmental impact of energy consumption created via mining. We know that validators stake their funds towards solving a block, like placing a bet, but what happens if someone tries to "cheat"?

In Ethereum's Proof-of-Stake algorithm (called Casper), what will happen, in the event of a bad actor, is that the funds belonging to anyone trying to do something nefarious will simply disappear! The system will erase them out of circulation. So, the incentive for a validator to participate in earnest is high, and the consequences for trying to "validate" a false transaction are high.

The Proof-of-Work and Proof-of-Stake models both ultimately strive for the same outcome: they want to validate blocks and add those blocks to the blockchain in such a way that the broader network is in consensus about the validity of those blocks. Both models, ideally, will achieve the same result through a different protocol.

As a potential investor and/or participant in the blockchain space, becoming familiar with different consensus models is a good way to deepen your understanding of how projects function in the real world. The shift in Ethereum's model from Proof-of-Work based on mining to Proof-of-Stake based on validation will further set Ethereum apart from Bitcoin in terms of its structure, but it is also worth examining some of the other ways in which these two technologies are already fundamentally quite different.

We have already mentioned that Ethereum, while it is a currency in part, is primarily a platform for developing decentralized applications. The idea of decentralized applications (often called "dApps") can be a little bit confusing, largely because it is a really new way of organizing information. Why do we need a blockchain-based platform to run applications? This is actually a question that many programmers are still exploring the answers to. One answer, however, has to do with a concept that is referred to in the world of programming as "state."

"State" basically just refers to the status of any given application or program at a certain point in time. One of the things that makes Ethereum's blockchain different than Bitcoin's is that "transactions" that happen on the Ethereum blockchain can actually trigger code to be executed. So, programs can be triggered to run as a result of transactions that happen on the Ethereum platform. Each time something changes within an application, that application's state changes. The Ethereum blockchain keeps a record of every state change that occurs within an application. For example, a smart contract can be paid when work is delivered entirely through the Ethereum blockchain.

If you're feeling a little bit lost, don't worry. Unless you plan on developing applications on the Ethereum platform, you really don't need to understand the technical aspects of state change. That being said, it is worth becoming familiar with these concepts if you plan get involved in the blockchain space as an investor or entrepreneur. To get a better idea of what Ethereum is capable of, it let's look at one of the decentralized apps being developed on the Ethereum platform.

Golem

Golem is one popular project based on the Ethereum framework. The idea is fairly simple. A lot of people have computers. A lot of people who have computers don't use them all of the time, and even when they are using them they often don't use them to their full capacity in terms of processing power. At the same time, there are a lot of fields where massive amounts of computing power are required to accomplish certain tasks. For example, rendering video is very costly in terms of computing power. It takes a long time and it can be pretty slow on a slow machine. Many scientific studies also require computationally intensive data analysis and other forms of high-level computer processing.

The Golem project is designed to allow people to essentially rent out their unused computer processing power to people who need it for projects. Using a decentralized structure, this means that people from all over the world can contribute small amounts of their computer power towards completing a computationally intensive task that would normally require a very powerful computer to accomplish.

By using a blockchain-based framework that allows for code to be executed when transactions occur, i.e. Ethereum, Golem is working towards creating what are essentially decentralized supercomputers that are accessible to anyone. Because the entire history of a program's state is recorded on the Ethereum blockchain, participants can ensure that nobody is using more power than they have paid for and vice-versa, as well as ensure other features concerning their transactions.

Golem also has its own digital currency, based on Ether, through which participants can buy and sell their resources, and, of course, which anyone can invest in regardless of whether or not they are participating in the project directly. Golem is widely considered to be one of the more popular and successful applications built on the Ethereum platform as of the time of this writing.

Ripple

We've already covered some of the ways in which Ethereum differs from Bitcoin. One thing that we have not yet noted is that Ethereum, unlike Bitcoin, is managed by a central team of known people. This group determines what happens with Ethereum, such as the move from Proof-of-Work to Proof-of-Stake, and therefore exercises a certain level of control over the platform in a way that is more centralized than Bitcoin. Even so, Ethereum is still an open blockchain platform, accessible to anyone.

Ripple is another example of a variation on blockchain technology. Ripple is twofold: both a cryptocurrency and a technology company in the blockchain space. Ripple's focus is less on peer-to-peer transactions and more on the financial industry itself, partnering with banks and financial institutions to integrate blockchain technology into their infrastructure.

Ripple remains somewhat controversial amongst cryptocurrency enthusiasts, but it does claim to solve some of the problems posed by Bitcoin. Most significantly, Ripple eliminates the waiting period associated with verification. Transactions can happen instantly. However, Ripple's consensus model differs from Bitcoin's "Proof of Work" model and instead relies on a centralized network of "trusted" servers, which poses some big questions for those whose interest in blockchain technology lies in the promise of decentralized architecture.

The concept of a distributed ledger as it is implemented via blockchain technology represents a fundamental reimagining of institutional organizations from a hierarchical model to a distributed network. For many investors, this is the key to the revolutionary potential of blockchain technology. The implications of decentralizing information are significant, and almost certainly have not yet been fully realized.

CHAPTER 5
IMPLICATIONS OF BLOCKCHAIN: BIG DATA, PRIVACY, AND PERSONAL DATA

As we enter an increasingly digital age, many of the practices that were developed prior to the Internet have simply been applied to the new framework of a networked world. Instead of writing letters, we now send e-mails, for example. At face value, the process doesn't seem that all that different. In some cases, it isn't.

Regardless of how you may feel about it, there is no denying that more and more things are becoming integrated into the Internet, hence the aptly titled notion of the "Internet of Things" (often abbreviated to IoT). Devices like heart-rate monitors, self-driving cars, and even refrigerators are making their way into the market. Of course, almost everyone is already accustomed to carrying a smart phone around at all times, regularly checking GPS information, updating social media feeds, managing financial transactions, and much more.

Almost every area of life that one can think of is wired into the web already, or has the potential to be in the near future. While there are many advantages to the bourgeoning revolution in "smart technology," there are also some major concerns and challenges.

While it may seem like things like social media networks, smart toasters, and FitBits are entirely different ideas, they actually have quite a bit in common.

Fundamentally, they all produce data: data about you. If you recall in the section on SHA-256, we noted that all digital data can ultimately be reduced to 0's and 1's. From that perspective, our heart rate and our Google search history are not ultimately all that different in terms. We all generate data constantly, whether it is telling Amazon's Alexa to order more paper towels, Googling pictures of baby sea lions, or tracking your workout schedule with an App or a wearable.

Where does this data go? Who *owns* this data? What can be learned about you by your trail of data? These questions quickly lead anyone bold enough to ask them into very uncomfortable territory. While getting to deep into the answer to this particular set of questions is beyond the scope of this book, it is worth scratching the surface. In short, there are huge multi-national companies that buy up your data and sell it to other companies. What do they do with it? Good question. Of course, they target ads based on your history. Sure. We all know that. What else, though? Part of what makes this avenue uncomfortable is that nobody really knows, and the space of data collection is loosely defined and loosely regulated.

Let's look at an example. Let's say, hypothetically, you found a little lump in your armpit one day. You are naturally a bit nervous, and you rush over to Google and spend several hours clicking around different websites to read articles about cancer. Now, let's say, hypothetically, that whatever company is sucking up your data gets their hands on this searching binge. Perhaps they also notice that you looked up a phone number for some doctor in the area who does cancer screenings. While you're at it, maybe it is time to start thinking about your health insurance policy, or to buy life insurance just incase?

Continuing the hypothetical situation, if an insurance provider were to buy your data, already parsed by some massive data broker, and see that you had been recently looking up information about cancer, what are the implications? Even if you have told nobody about the lump, even if you have not been evaluated by a doctor or diagnosed, could this potential insurer infer things from your data history when deciding on your premium rate, or whether to offer insurance to you at all?

This is just one example of a wide range of ethical and legal dilemmas that arise when we really begin thinking about the implications of our data, how it is mined, who "owns it," and who has access to it.

The more integrated technology becomes into society and all levels of life, and the more pervasive networks become, the greater the volume and variety of data about all of us. What movies and music we stream, our shopping history, political leanings, sexual preferences, connections on social networks, devices we use, and much more is information that is often being collected as a result of blindly checking a user agreement box in order to use a particular service.

Ok, that's creepy, but what does it have to do with blockchain technology? Good question. The relationship between privacy and technology is an issue that spans many industries and contemporary debates.

For many enthusiasts of both cryptocurrencies and blockchain technology, privacy is a major concern. When it comes to the concept of "privacy," many observers, including major media outlets, make the assumption that "the only people who care about privacy are those with something to hide." This has led to a great deal of reporting on crytocurrencies, in particular, suggesting that the primary appeal of these technologies is that they enable criminal activity. As more and more areas of life become connected to the Internet, it seems far-fetched to suggest that desiring more control over one's personal data, transactions, and asset management constitutes or implies criminal behavior. Many privacy advocates argue that privacy is essential to both individual welfare and a functional democracy.

Rather than relying on centralized institutions to provide services in exchange for ownership over our data, blockchain-based models are beginning to emerge that shift information to a secure, trustless, decentralized structure. ("Trustless" here means that participants do not need to put their trust in a centralized institution to mediate transactions, keep records, distribute wealth, store data, etc.).

The implications for blockchain in spaces like managing personal information, such as health records, are extremely promising and beginning to gain a lot of attention from investors, entrepreneurs, major corporations, and government entities.

Regardless of your feelings on the subject of privacy, it is worth noting, from an investment perspective, that several notable cryptocurrencies have emerged with an emphasis on privacy as a defining factor. The ability to make completely anonymous transactions that are also totally secure has elevated several currencies to the forefront of the cryptocurrency space, including Monero,

ZCash, and Dash. While none of these have reached quite the height of Bitcoin or Ethereum in terms of widespread adoption, all three of these are among the top 50 cryptocurrencies in terms of market value. We can infer from their success that enough people see value in anonymity to make these currencies competitive players in the larger cryptocurrency market, as well as the general blockchain space.

Profiting from Blockchain Technologies

It is important to remember that blockchain technology is still very new. The implications of secure distributed ledgers and decentralized peer-to-peer systems of this variety are not yet fully realized. As with any frontier space, even in the digital realm, there are a lot of opportunities. Of course, the nature of frontiers is that they are unexplored territory, and where there is potential for opportunity there is also a higher risk factor than one might encounter in tamer and more regulated environments.

While much of the blockchain space is a "wild west," major players and industry leaders from numerous fields are beginning to invest in and explore blockchain technology. Big technology companies such as IBM and Microsoft are beginning to explore blockchains, along with numerous banks, particularly in Europe and Asia.

Even governments in many parts of the world are beginning to implement blockchains to manage public services and records. Estonia, for example, issues citizens cryptographically secure ID cards, managed by a blockchain, that allow access to various public services. The government of Georgia is using blockchain technology to manage land titles and validate property transactions. The UN recently completed a trial program using the Ethereum blockchain to manage distribution of food aid to 10,000 refugees.

Over the past few years, numerous hedge funds dealing in cryptocurrencies and blockchain applications have sprung up all over the world, and many Wall Street speculators have fixed their attention on the blockchain space. In 2016, Overstock, one of the largest online retailers in the US, released a blockchain-based platform for equities trading. Numerous startups have emerged that use blockchains to manage peer-to-peer micropayments at extremely low rates. In some cases these enable international transfers and access to cash pickups, which allows unbanked individuals to send and receive payments.

New developments are happening on a daily basis in the blockchain space. For those interested in diving in, getting involved, and profiting from these emerging technologies, the single most important thing you can do is to stay informed: Read white papers, join online communities, and explore the different projects gaining traction around blockchain technology. The more familiar you are with the space, the easier it will be to make informed decisions about which projects to invest in.

As a practical matter, broadly speaking, there are two general directions you can go in terms of investing in blockchain technology: cryptocurrencies and everything else. These are by no means mutually exclusive, and as we have seen with projects like Ethereum and Ripple, there is often some overlap between the two, or the integration of a digital token into a particular blockchain application.

Within the cryptocurrency space, active online marketplaces and exchanges exist with a trading culture similar to traditional stock exchanges. People trade fiat currency for cryptocurrencies as well as trading one cryptocurrency for another, striving to making a profit by investing in currencies that they think will increase in value.

Most cyrptocurrency exchanges deal primarily in Bitcoin. In order to buy into other cryptocurrencies, you almost always need to have some Bitcoin to exchange, although some currencies and exchanges allow for a direct exchange between fiat and "altcoins," a common term for cryptocurrencies other than Bitcoin. You can buy Bitcoin through several online exchanges or from an increasing number of Bitcoin ATM's that are available in various locations throughout the world.

You may choose to actively trade between different cryptocurrencies, or simply buy into Bitcoin and/or altcoins that you believe are promising and hold on to them with the assumption that they will increase in value over time. This is one way to get involved with what is currently the most active environment for blockchain applications. If you're lucky, you could end up as an "early investor" in a technology that really takes off.

Many people have entered the cryptocurrency space with precisely that hope, especially after hearing about the success of Bitcoin. If you are new to blockchain-based digital currencies, it is important to understand that this is an extremely volatile space. It is not uncommon to see huge spikes and drops in value throughout the course of a few hours, awhile it is possible to make a lot of money if you play your cards right, it is also easy to lose money.

Being aware of the risks and making smart investments in cryptocurrencies is arguably the most direct route towards profiting from blockchain technology. It is certainly the easiest. For people that don't necessarily have much capital to invest, the prospect of mining can sound pretty appealing. We've already discussed some of the challenges associated with mining Bitcoin: you need to buy specialized equipment, electricity costs, the need for massive computer power, etc. If you're low on capital, investing in a Bitcoin mining operation is probably not the best option.

However, there are many other cryptocurrencies that can be mined with considerably less of a barrier to entry. For those who are willing to learn what it takes convert a spare computer into a mining rig, the ability to earn coins through mining can be a potential way to generate passive income through validating blockchain transactions.

Blockchain technology originated in the cryptocurrency space, and much of the early development of blockchain applications has been in relation to digital assets and financial transactions. In terms of profiting from blockchain technology, becoming involved with cryptocurrencies is one popular avenue, but it is not the only gig in town.   Increasingly, as blockchain finds its way into new fields, a savvy investor can find many fascinating offshoots that could very well grow into massive projects with global implications and take the future by storm. Investing in companies, developers, and technology that are exploring the possibilities of blockchain is gaining rapid popularity with everyone from Silicon Valley entrepreneurs to Wall Street executives.

Of course, nobody knows for certain which blockchain-based application will be "the next Google." Any potential investor will inevitably face the challenge of gauging which initiatives are over-hyped versus which are promising underdogs, which are revolutionary platforms versus cheap imitations. While there is no crystal ball that can predict the future, you can bolster your odds of picking a winner by doing research and asking the right questions. Some important questions to ask when considering whether a project has a good chance of success include:

- What problem does the technology solve (Does incorporating a blockchain actually make sense in this situation? Is this the best solution?)

- Is this project actually functional? Is it live and being used currently or is it an idea that has not yet been built? If it hasn't been built, how can you be sure that it will actually accomplish what it promises?

- How is the blockchain structured? (For example, if the founder controls 90% of the nodes on the network, what might that say about the company?)

- What is their consensus algorithm? Proof-of-Work? Proof-of-Stake? Something else? Why did they choose this system and how is it implemented.

- Is it scalable? Could this system meet the demands of a large user base?

- How does anonymity factor into this application? Is that significant?

- Is this platform secure? How is security guaranteed? Is there "trust" involved in a centralized body? What kind of encryption are they using?

- Is the blockchain open and visible to anybody?

- Is the project's code open-source? (If it's not, why not? How will we be able to determine how decisions are made, transactions are deemed valid, and exactly what is being executed when we use this platform?)

- Who is behind this project? Is the development team qualified and reputable? Have they been involved with previous projects that failed? Why did those fail?

- Are other projects doing something similar? What makes this one the best?

- Do you believe in this project? Are you excited about it?

This laundry list of questions is by no means exhaustive, but if you are thinking about investing serious money in blockchain technology these considerations are a good place to begin. With the increasing attention of several major industries aimed towards blockchain technology, it should not come as a surprise that many entrepreneurs have taken notice of the potential for big money in developing blockchain applications. Needless to say, not all of these applications are going to succeed and some are more promising than others. Some projects can be noble efforts that simply don't have the best solution to a common problem; others may be outright scams.

Take time to become familiar with the buzzwords and jargon of the blockchain space. When a new company claims to deliver a blockchain platform that is "100% scalable," a wise investor will likely ask exactly how they have managed to accomplish this, rather than taking the company's word at face value. More often than not, you may find that bold claims like "100% scalable" are closer to "future goals" than to the current reality.

It is no secret that marketing hype can play a huge role in how "popular" something becomes. Cryptocurrencies and blockchain-based companies are no exception, and marketing can have a real impact on how a player in this space is valued. Maybe a project lives up to the hype, but it is generally a good idea to approach potential investments in this space with a dose of healthy skepticism. Alternatively, some of the most innovative and promising blockchain initiatives may be tiny start-ups with small budgets that do not have fancy websites and are not getting a huge amount of public attention.

By staying informed, looking at a wide variety of projects, figuring out which problems you think could be most successfully solved by blockchain technology, and gaining exposure to alternative points of view you can develop an in-depth understanding of the blockchain space. While there are no guarantees when it comes to investing, knowing what to look for goes a long way towards helping you will make smart decisions. Blockchain is still in the early days, and making smart decisions now definitely has the potential to lead to major profits.

Limitations & Challenges of Blockchain Technology

It is one thing to understand the concept of a blockchain; it is another thing to actually build one that scales over time, remains secure, and functions in real-world scenarios. Even if you manage to accomplish all of that, the challenge of getting people to actually invest in and use your technology can prove significant. For those interested in becoming involved with blockchain space, it is worth taking some time to look at some of the potential downsides, struggles, and limitations that blockchain technology currently faces.

Speed

One of the biggest challenges facing Bitcoin, and other blockchains using a Proof-of-Work model based on Bitcoin, is speed. Because mining a block is so resource intensive and involves so much trial and error in terms of finding the proper nonce to solve a block, it takes around 10 minutes for every new block to be mined.

Not only does this utilize a massive amount of electricity, but it also means that transactions are not verified instantaneously. In fact, it can take quite awhile to see your transaction move from "pending" to "verified". As a practical matter, this makes it difficult to buy something with Bitcoin in many situations. Most people don't want to wait around at a store for an hour while their transaction goes through. Furthermore, most merchants don't want to wait to see their money come through.

Despite this issue, the number of vendors willing to accept Bitcoin is growing on a daily basis. As more implementations of blockchain technology develop, different approaches are being taken to handle the speed of transaction and verification. Ripple, for example, offers instantaneous transactions but many critics have concerns about the centralization of the underlying protocol backing the technology that makes this kind of speed possible.

As a potential investor in a new technology, it is important to ask both how this is being addressed and examine whether security is being sacrificed to maximize speed. This is certainly not always the case, but it is something to watch out for when looking into new blockchain frameworks.

Scaling

Scaling is another one of the most notable issues currently facing blockchain implementations. If you visualize the blockchain exactly as it sounds, as a long chain of blocks, you can imagine that as more transactions occur and more blocks are added the chain, the chain gets longer and longer.

Part of what makes a blockchain work is that multiple copies of it are stored and updated across a decentralized network. In theory, when a chain gets bigger, it will inevitably take up more and more space. If a chain were to get so big that it required a huge amount of storage space, those who didn't have ample room to store the chain would no longer be able to participate in the network. Thus, over time, only giant servers would suffice to store the enormous chain, leading us back the very sort of centralized model that blockchain technology was ultimately designed to avoid.

Scaling is a major problem that is being addressed in a variety of ways by innovators in the cryptocurrency and blockchain space. The "Lightning Network" is one method that has been introduced as a promising potential solution to current scaling problems faced by blockchain applications.

The Lightning Network works by allowing peer-to-peer micro-transactions to happen instantaneously using blockchain smart contracts, but without adding individual transactions to the main blockchain. The Lightning Network also supports "atomic swaps" between different blockchains, i.e. from one cryptocurrency to another, so long as those chains support the same cryptographic hash functions. By combining the Bitcoin blockchain with its own, in-house, scripting language to manage smart contracts, the Lightning Network is one example of a blockchain-based solution to the problem of blockchain scaling. This is one example of how this technology builds upon itself to develop new implementations on top of the existing architecture.

Quantum Computing

Quantum computers might sound like science fiction, but they are not far from becoming a reality. Without getting into the "how" of quantum computing, what we need to look at in relation to blockchain technology is the "what." What does quantum computing mean for us, generally, and what are the implications for blockchain tech?

In a nutshell, the promise of quantum computing is incredible speed and incredible power. As of now, if we look at the example of Bitcoin, we know that blocks are "mined" by a decentralized network of machines that work to verify Bitcoin transactions by solving complex math problems in exchange for a small amount of Bitcoin. When the problem is solved and the transaction is verified, a block is added to the chain.

Quantum computers would be able to solve these math problems at a rate infinitely faster than anything currently in existence. That's problem number one.

Problem number two arises when we think about the model of majority consensus that governs the Bitcoin protocol. In order to modify the blockchain, one would have to alter the record on over 50% of copies stored all around the world. Today, the kind of processing power required to do that makes hacking the blockchain effectively impossible. Quantum computing has the potential change that, although at the moment this risk remains theoretical.

CHAPTER 6
THE HUMAN TOUCH: OR, THE 51% PROBLEM

One of the central pillars of blockchain technology is the ability to conduct transactions in a trustless environment without needing a "middle-man." In laymen's terms, we ultimately put our trust in an unbiased mathematical process carried out by computers rather than in human beings. We are guaranteed a form of security that is theoretically as free as possible from human tampering.

Of course, it is impossible to discount human beings completely. The power of a decentralized application that relies on computational verification marks a significant paradigm shift from a top-down hierarchy towards a distributed network. However, when we look at the Bitcoin blockchain we can see that the consensus model requires a majority to agree in order to verify a block. 51% of miners constitute a majority.

What happens if, as the expenses of mining increase along with the ever-growing blockchain, miners consolidate their influence into larger and larger pools? This concern is not entirely theoretical. As of the time of this writing, almost 50% of all Bitcoin blocks are estimated to be mined by two large mining pools.

To execute what is known as a "51% attack," a single entity would have to contribute 51% or more of the entire bitcoin networks mining hashrate. This would require an almost unfathomable amount of computer power, which would equate to an equally unfathomable electricity cost. Realistically, most governments do not even possess the resources to execute a 51% attack on Bitcoin. It would be incredibly difficult, but it is not necessarily impossible. If it did happen, the attacker would not really be able to take complete control over the network. They would be able to prevent new transactions from being validated, but they could not reverse transactions that were already recorded on the blockchain, steal Bitcoins from other people's wallets or create new Bitcoins at will.

The 51% problem is something that any decentralized structure built on a similar model will need to contend with. Some advocates of Proof-of-Stake consensus suggest that this model offers more robust security against a 51% attack.

All emerging industries and new technologies face challenges, and blockchains are no exception. An entire generation of entrepreneurs, developers, and professionals is emerging in the blockchain space, and for those who believe in the revolutionary potential of this technology it is a land of opportunity.

The Future of Blockchain

We've covered several foundational concepts throughout the course of this book in relation to blockchain technology. As the world becomes more and more interconnected through networked technology, and the amount of data we generate grows in both quantity and form, there is an increasing demand and opportunity for new models of organization to handle the interface of digital and material life. Blockchain's usage of a distributed ledger and the potential for creating decentralized rather than hierarchical structures in a way that is secure, trustless, and open marks a revolutionary step towards reimagining the way many of today's dominant institutions operate.

As with any new technology, there are competing ideologies, varying implementations, and a number of challenges that are present in the blockchain space. Whether the Bitcoin blockchain will continue to be the dominant blockchain model and Bitcoin will continue as the most popular cryptocurrency is something that only time will tell. There is, undoubtedly, a lot of room to grow when it comes to realizing the full potential of blockchain technology in terms of creating institutional transparency, decentralized networks, peer-to-peer transactions, asset management, and much more. Industries ranging from healthcare, finance, and social media to retail, airlines, and manufacturing have all begun to explore the potential for integrating with blockchain-based systems. Governments, banks, and organizations have already begun to implement blockchain systems to manage transactions, access to public services, and the distribution of humanitarian aid.

Whether you are excited by the ideological implications of decentralized networks radically transforming the landscape of hierarchical institutions on a global scale or you are an investor eager to get on board with the next big thing, blockchain technology is markedly promising. Blockchain is unquestionably the way of the future. Despite the huge uptick in interest in blockchain technology over the past few years, we are still very much in the early stages of this space. Even if you're completely new to blockchain today, in five or ten years you could very likely be considered an "early adopter" of most disruptive technology since the advent of the Internet.

CONCLUSION

I'd like to thank you for purchasing this book and I commend you on taking the initiative to take the time and learn about blockchain technology.

I hope this short read was able to help you to get a basic understanding of exactly what cryptocurrency and the Blockchain is, sparking your interest to do some further research and start your journey toward sovereignty.

The next step is to get active on the message forums and with the resources mentioned in this book.

Finally, if you enjoyed this book then I'd like to ask if would you be kind enough to leave a review for Amazon?

It will be highly appreciated.

Thank you and good luck!

© Copyright 2017 by – Artemis Caro - All rights reserved.

This document is geared towards providing exact and reliable information in regards to the topic and issue covered. The publication is sold with the idea that the publisher is not required to render accounting, officially permitted, or otherwise, qualified services. If advice is necessary, legal or professional, a practiced individual in the profession should be ordered.

- From a Declaration of Principles which was accepted and approved equally by a Committee of the American Bar Association and a Committee of Publishers and Associations.

In no way is it legal to reproduce, duplicate, or transmit any part of this document in either electronic means or in printed format. Recording of this publication is strictly prohibited and any storage of this document is not allowed unless with written permission from the publisher. All rights reserved.

The information provided herein is stated to be truthful and consistent, in that any liability, in terms of inattention or otherwise, by any usage or abuse of any policies, processes, or directions contained within is the solitary and utter responsibility of the recipient reader. Under no circumstances will any legal responsibility or blame be held against the publisher or author for any reparation, damages, or monetary loss due to the information herein, either directly or indirectly.

Respective authors own all copyrights not held by the publisher.

The information herein is offered for informational purposes solely, and is universal as so. The presentation of the information is without contract or any type of guarantee assurance.

The trademarks that are used are without any consent, and the publication of the trademark is without permission or backing by the trademark owner. All trademarks and brands within this book are for clarifying purposes only and are the owned by the owners themselves, not affiliated with this document.

CPSIA information can be obtained
at www.ICGtesting.com
Printed in the USA
LVHW01s0406061117
555120LV00001B/3/P